STATE
OF THE UNION
ADDRESSES

BY

JOHN F. KENNEDY

1st WORLD
LIBRARY
Literary Society

State of The Union Addresses

John F Kennedy

© 1st World Library – Literary Society, 2004
PO Box 2211
Fairfield, IA 52556
www.1stworldlibrary.org
First Edition

LCCN: 2003195026

ISBN: 1-59540-309-4

Purchase *"The State of The Union Adresses"*
as a traditional bound book at:
www.1stWorldLibrary.org/purchase.asp?ISBN=1-59540-309-4

1st World Library Literary Society is a nonprofit
organization dedicated to promoting literacy by:

- Creating a free internet library accessible from any
computer worldwide.
- Hosting writing competitions and offering book
publishing scholarships.

Readers interested in supporting literacy
through sponsorship, donations or
membership please contact:
literacy@1stworldlibrary.org
Check us out at: www.1stworldlibrary.org

State of The Union Addresses
contributed by the Charles Family
in support of
1st World Library - Literary Society

State of the Union Address
John F. Kennedy
January 30, 1961

Mr. Speaker, Mr. Vice President, Members of the Congress:

It is a pleasure to return from whence I came. You are among my oldest friends in Washington - and this House is my oldest home. It was here, more than 14 years ago, that I first took the oath of Federal office. It was here, for 14 years, that I gained both knowledge and inspiration from members of both parties in both Houses - from your wise and generous leaders - and from the pronouncements which I can vividly recall, sitting where you now sit - including the programs of two great Presidents, the undimmed eloquence of Churchill, the soaring idealism of Nehru, the steadfast words of General de Gaulle. To speak from this same historic rostrum is a sobering experience. To be back among so many friends is a happy one.

I am confident that that friendship will continue. Our Constitution wisely assigns both joint and separate roles to each branch of the government; and a President and a Congress who hold each other in mutual respect will neither permit nor attempt any trespass. For my part, I shall withhold from neither the Congress nor the people any fact or report, past, present, or future, which is necessary for an informed judgment of our conduct and hazards. I shall neither shift the burden of executive decisions to the Congress, nor avoid responsibility for the outcome of those decisions.

I speak today in an hour of national peril and national opportunity. Before my term has ended, we shall have to test anew whether a nation organized and governed such as ours can endure. The outcome is by no means certain. The answers are by no means clear. All of us together - this Administration, this Congress, this nation - must forge those answers.

But today, were I to offer - after little more than a week in office - detailed legislation to remedy every national ill, the Congress would rightly wonder whether the desire for speed had replaced the duty of responsibility.

My remarks, therefore, will be limited. But they will also be candid. To state the facts frankly is not to despair the future nor indict the past. The prudent heir takes careful inventory of his legacies, and gives a faithful accounting to those whom he owes an obligation of trust. And, while the occasion does not call for another recital of our blessings and assets, we do have no greater asset than the willingness of a free and determined people, through its elected officials, to face all problems frankly and meet all dangers free from panic or fear.

I.

The present state of our economy is disturbing. We take office in the wake of seven months of recession, three and one-half years of slack, seven years of diminished economic growth, and nine years of falling farm income.

Business bankruptcies have reached their highest level since the Great Depression. Since 1951 farm income has been squeezed down by 25 percent. Save for a brief period in 1958, insured unemployment is at the highest peak in our history. Of some five and one-half million Americans who are without jobs, more than one million have been searching for work for more than four months. And during each month some 150,000 workers are exhausting their already meager jobless benefit rights.

Nearly one-eighth of those who are without jobs live almost without hope in nearly one hundred especially depressed and troubled areas. The rest include new school graduates unable to use their talents, farmers forced to give up their part-time jobs which helped balance their family budgets, skilled and unskilled workers laid off in such important industries as metals, machinery, automobiles and apparel.

Our recovery from the 1958 recession, moreover, was anemic and incomplete. Our Gross National Product never regained its full potential. Unemployment never returned to normal levels. Maximum use of our national industrial capacity was never restored.

In short, the American economy is in trouble. The most

resourceful industrialized country on earth ranks among the last in the rate of economic growth. Since last spring our economic growth rate has actually receded. Business investment is in a decline. Profits have fallen below predicted levels. Construction is off. A million unsold automobiles are in inventory. Fewer people are working - and the average work week has shrunk well below 40 hours. Yet prices have continued to rise - so that now too many Americans have less to spend for items that cost more to buy.

Economic prophecy is at best an uncertain art - as demonstrated by the prediction one year ago from this same podium that 1960 would be, and I quote, "the most prosperous year in our history." Nevertheless, forecasts of continued slack and only slightly reduced unemployment through 1961 and 1962 have been made with alarming unanimity - and this Administration does not intend to stand helplessly by.

We cannot afford to waste idle hours and empty plants while awaiting the end of the recession. We must show the world what a free economy can do - to reduce unemployment, to put unused capacity to work, to spur new productivity, and to foster higher economic growth within a range of sound fiscal policies and relative price stability.

I will propose to the Congress within the next 14 days measures to improve unemployment compensation through temporary increases in duration on a self-supporting basis - to provide more food for the families of the unemployed, and to aid their needy children - to redevelop our areas of chronic labor surplus - to expand the services of the U.S. Employment Offices - to stimulate housing and construction - to secure more purchasing power for our lowest paid workers by raising and expanding the minimum wage - to offer tax incentives for sound plant investment - to increase the development of our natural resources - to encourage price stability - and to take other steps aimed at insuring a prompt recovery and paving the way for increased long-range growth. This is not a partisan program concentrating on our weaknesses - it is, I hope, a national program to realize our national strength.

II.

Efficient expansion at home, stimulating the new plant and technology that can make our goods more competitive, is also the key to the international balance of payments problem. Laying aside all alarmist talk and panicky solutions, let us put that knotty problem in its proper perspective.

It is true that, since 1958, the gap between the dollars we spend or invest abroad and the dollars returned to us has substantially widened. This overall deficit in our balance of payments increased by nearly $11 billion in the 3 years - and holders of dollars abroad converted them to gold in such a quantity as to cause a total outflow of nearly $5 billion of gold from our reserve. The 1959 deficit was caused in large part by the failure of our exports to penetrate foreign markets - the result both of restrictions on our goods and our own uncompetitive prices. The 1960 deficit, on the other hand, was more the result of an increase in private capital outflow seeking new opportunity, higher return or speculative advantage abroad.

Meanwhile this country has continued to bear more than its share of the West's military and foreign aid obligations. Under existing policies, another deficit of $2 billion is predicted for 1961 - and individuals in those countries whose dollar position once depended on these deficits for improvement now wonder aloud whether our gold reserves will remain sufficient to meet our own obligations.

All this is cause for concern - but it is not cause for panic. For our monetary and financial position remains exceedingly strong. Including our drawing rights in the International Monetary Fund and the gold reserve held as backing for our currency and Federal Reserve deposits, we have some $22 billion in total gold stocks and other international monetary reserves available - and I now pledge that their full strength stands behind the value of the dollar for use if needed.

Moreover, we hold large assets abroad - the total owed this nation far exceeds the claims upon our reserves - and our exports once again substantially exceed our imports.

In short, we need not - and we shall not - take any action to increase the dollar price of gold from $35 an ounce - to impose exchange controls - to reduce our anti-recession efforts - to fall back on restrictive trade policies - or to weaken our commitments around the world.

This Administration will not distort the value of the dollar in any fashion. And this is a commitment.

Prudence and good sense do require, however, that new steps be taken to ease the payments deficit and prevent any gold crisis. Our success in world affairs has long depended in part upon foreign confidence in our ability to pay. A series of executive orders, legislative remedies and cooperative efforts with our allies will get underway immediately - aimed at attracting foreign investment and travel to this country - promoting American exports, at stable prices and with more liberal government guarantees and financing - curbing tax and customs loopholes that encourage undue spending of private dollars abroad - and (through OECD, NATO and otherwise) sharing with our allies all efforts to provide for the common defense of the free world and the hopes for growth of the less developed lands. While the current deficit lasts, ways will be found to ease our dollar outlays abroad without placing the full burden on the families of men whom we have asked to serve our Flag overseas.

In short, whatever is required will be done to back up all our efforts abroad, and to make certain that, in the future as in the past, the dollar is as "sound as a dollar."

III.

But more than our exchange of international payments is out of balance. The current Federal budget for fiscal 1961 is almost certain to show a net deficit. The budget already submitted for fiscal 1962 will remain in balance only if the Congress enacts all the revenue measures requested - and only if an earlier and sharper up-turn in the economy than my economic advisers now think likely produces the tax revenues estimated. Nevertheless, a new Administration must of necessity build on the spending and revenue estimates already submitted. Within that framework, barring the development of urgent national defense needs or a worsening of the economy, it is my current intention to advocate a program of expenditures which, including revenues from a stimulation of the economy, will not of and by themselves unbalance the earlier Budget.

However, we will do what must be done. For our national household is cluttered with unfinished and neglected tasks. Our cities are being engulfed in squalor. Twelve long years after Congress declared our goal to be "a decent home and a suitable environment for every American family," we still have 25 million Americans living in substandard homes. A new housing program under a new Housing and Urban Affairs Department will be needed this year.

Our classrooms contain 2 million more children than they can properly have room for, taught by 90,000 teachers not properly qualified to teach. One third of our most promising high school graduates are financially unable to continue the development of their talents. The war babies of the 1940's, who over-crowded our schools in the 1950's, are now descending in 1960 upon our colleges - with two college students for every one, ten years from now - and our colleges are ill prepared. We lack the scientists, the engineers and the teachers our world obligations require. We have neglected oceanography, saline water conversion, and the basic research that lies at the root of all progress. Federal grants for both higher and public school education can no longer be delayed.

Medical research has achieved new wonders - but these wonders are too often beyond the reach of too many people, owing to a lack of income (particularly among the aged), a lack of hospital beds, a lack of nursing homes and a lack of doctors and dentists. Measures to provide health care for the aged under Social Security, and to increase the supply of both facilities and personnel, must be undertaken this year.

Our supply of clean water is dwindling. Organized and juvenile crimes cost the taxpayers millions of dollars each year, making it essential that we have improved enforcement and new legislative safeguards. The denial of constitutional rights to some of our fellow Americans on account of race - at the ballot box and elsewhere - disturbs the national conscience, and subjects us to the charge of world opinion that our democracy is not equal to the high promise of our heritage. Morality in private business has not been sufficiently spurred by morality in public business. A host of problems and projects in all 50 States, though not possible to include in this Message, deserves - and will receive - the attention of both the Congress and the Executive Branch. On most of these matters, Messages will be sent to the Congress within the next two weeks.

IV.

But all these problems pale when placed beside those which confront us around the world. No man entering upon this office, regardless of his party, regardless of his previous service in Washington, could fail to be staggered upon learning - even in this brief 10 day period - the harsh enormity of the trials through which we must pass in the next four years. Each day the crises multiply. Each day their solution grows more difficult. Each day we draw nearer the hour of maximum danger, as weapons spread and hostile forces grow stronger. I feel I must inform the Congress that our analyses over the last ten days make it clear that - in each of the principal areas of crisis - the tide of events has been running out and time has not been our friend.

In Asia, the relentless pressures of the Chinese Communists menace the security of the entire area - from the borders of India and South Viet Nam to the jungles of Laos, struggling to protect its newly-won independence. We seek in Laos what we seek in all Asia, and, indeed, in all of the world - freedom for the people and independence for the government. And this Nation shall persevere in our pursuit of these objectives.

In Africa, the Congo has been brutally torn by civil strife, political unrest and public disorder. We shall continue to support the heroic efforts of the United Nations to restore peace and order - efforts which are now endangered by mounting tensions, unsolved problems, and decreasing support from many member states.

In Latin America, Communist agents seeking to exploit that region's peaceful revolution of hope have established a base on Cuba, only 90 miles from our shores. Our objection with Cuba is not over the people's drive for a better life. Our objection is to their domination by foreign and domestic tyrannies. Cuban social and economic reform should be encouraged. Questions of economic and trade policy can always be negotiated. But Communist domination in this Hemisphere can never be negotiated.

We are pledged to work with our sister Republics to free the Americas of all such foreign domination and all tyranny, working toward the goal of a free hemisphere of free governments, extending from Cape Horn to the Arctic Circle.

In Europe our alliances are unfulfilled and in some disarray. The unity of NATO has been weakened by economic rivalry and partially eroded by national interest. It has not yet fully mobilized its resources nor fully achieved a common outlook. Yet no Atlantic power can meet on its own the mutual problems now facing us in defense, foreign aid, monetary reserves, and a host of other areas; and our close ties with those whose hopes and interests we share are among this Nation's most powerful assets.

Our greatest challenge is still the world that lies beyond the Cold War - but the first great obstacle is still our relations with the Soviet Union and Communist China. We must never be lulled into believing that either power has yielded its ambitions for world domination - ambitions which they forcefully restated only a short time ago. On the contrary, our task is to convince them that aggression and subversion will not be profitable routes to pursue these ends. Open and peaceful competition - for prestige, for markets, for scientific achievement, even for men's minds - is something else again. For if Freedom and Communism were to compete for man's allegiance in a world at peace, I would look to the future with ever increasing confidence.

To meet this array of challenges - to fulfill the role we cannot avoid on the world scene - we must reexamine and revise our whole arsenal of tools: military, economic and political.

One must not overshadow the other. On the Presidential Coat of Arms, the American eagle holds in his right talon the olive branch, while in his left he holds a bundle of arrows. We intend to give equal attention to both.

First, we must strengthen our military tools. We are moving into a period of uncertain risk and great commitment in which both the military and diplomatic possibilities require a Free World force so powerful as to make any aggression clearly futile. Yet in the past, lack of a consistent, coherent military strategy, the absence of basic assumptions about our national requirements and the faulty estimates and duplication arising from inter-service rivalries have all made it difficult to assess accurately how adequate - or inadequate - our defenses really are.

I have, therefore, instructed the Secretary of Defense to reappraise our entire defense strategy - our ability to fulfill our commitments - the effectiveness, vulnerability, and dispersal of our strategic bases, forces and warning systems - the efficiency and economy of our operation and organization - the elimination of obsolete bases and installations - and the adequacy, modernization and mobility of our present conventional and nuclear forces and weapons systems in the light of present and future dangers. I have asked for preliminary conclusions by the end of February -

and I then shall recommend whatever legislative, budgetary or executive action is needed in the light of these conclusions.

In the meantime, I have asked the Defense Secretary to initiate immediately three new steps most clearly needed now:

First, I have directed prompt attention to increase our air-lift capacity. Obtaining additional air transport mobility - and obtaining it now - will better assure the ability of our conventional forces to respond, with discrimination and speed, to any problem at any spot on the globe at any moment's notice. In particular it will enable us to meet any deliberate effort to avoid or divert our forces by starting limited wars in widely scattered parts of the globe.

(b) I have directed prompt action to step up our Polaris submarine program. Using unobligated ship-building funds now (to let contracts originally scheduled for the next fiscal year) will build and place on station - at least nine months earlier than planned - substantially more units of a crucial deterrent - a fleet that will never attack first, but possess sufficient powers of retaliation, concealed beneath the seas, to discourage any aggressor from launching an attack upon our security.

(c) I have directed prompt action to accelerate our entire missile program. Until the Secretary of Defense's reappraisal is completed, the emphasis here will be largely on improved organization and decision-making - on cutting down the wasteful duplications and the time-lag that have handicapped our whole family of missiles. If we are to keep the peace, we need an invulnerable missile force powerful enough to deter any aggressor from even threatening an attack that he would know could not destroy enough of our force to prevent his own destruction. For as I said upon taking the oath of office: "Only when our arms are sufficient beyond doubt can we be certain beyond doubt that they will never be employed."

Secondly, we must improve our economic tools. Our role is essential and unavoidable in the construction of a sound and expanding economy for the entire non-communist world, helping other nations build the strength to meet their own problems, to satisfy their own aspirations - to surmount their own dangers. The problems in achieving this goal are towering and unprecedented - the response must be towering and unprecedented as well, much as Lend-Lease and the Marshall Plan were in earlier years, which brought such fruitful results.

(a) I intend to ask the Congress for authority to establish a new and more effective program for assisting the economic, educational and social development of other countries and continents. That program must stimulate and take more effectively into account the contributions of our allies, and provide central policy direction for all our own programs that now so often overlap, conflict or diffuse our energies and resources. Such a program, compared to past programs, will require

- more flexibility for short run emergencies

- more commitment to long term development

- new attention to education at all levels

- greater emphasis on the recipient nation's role, their effort, their purpose, with greater social justice for their people, broader distribution and participation by their people and more efficient public administration and more efficient tax systems of their own

- and orderly planning for national and regional development instead of a piecemeal approach.

I hope the Senate will take early action approving the Convention establishing the Organization for Economic Cooperation and Development. This will be an important instrument in sharing with our allies this development effort - working toward the time when each nation will contribute in proportion to its ability to pay. For, while we are prepared to assume our full share of these huge burdens, we cannot and must not be expected to bear them alone.

To our sister republics to the south, we have pledged a new alliance for progress - alianza para progreso. Our goal is a free and prosperous Latin America, realizing for all its states and all its citizens a degree of economic and social progress that matches their historic contributions of culture, intellect and liberty. To start this nation's role at this time in that alliance of neighbors, I am recommending the following:

- That the Congress appropriate in full the $500 million fund pledged by the Act of Bogota, to be used not as an instrument of the Cold War, but as a first step in the sound development of the Americas.

- That a new Inter-Departmental Task Force be established under the leadership of the Department of State, to coordinate at the highest level all policies and programs of concern to the Americas.

- That our delegates to the OAS, working with those of other members, strengthen that body as an instrument to preserve the peace and to prevent foreign domination anywhere in the Hemisphere.

- That, in cooperation with other nations, we launch a new hemispheric attack on illiteracy and inadequate educational opportunities to all levels; and, finally,

- That a Food-for-Peace mission be sent immediately to Latin America to explore ways in which our vast food abundance can be used to help end hunger and malnutrition in certain areas of suffering in our own hemisphere.

This Administration is expanding its Food-for-Peace Program in every possible way. The product of our abundance must be used more effectively to relieve hunger and help economic growth in all corners of the globe. And I have asked the Director of this Program to recommend additional ways in which these surpluses can advance the interests of world peace - including the establishment of world food reserves.

An even more valuable national asset is our reservoir of dedicated men and women - not only on our college campuses but in every age group - who have indicated their desire to contribute their skills, their efforts, and a part of their lives to the fight for world order. We can mobilize this talent through the formation of a National Peace Corps, enlisting the services of all those with the desire and capacity to help foreign lands meet their urgent needs for trained personnel.

Finally, while our attention is centered on the development of the non-communist world, we must never forget our hopes for the ultimate freedom and welfare of the Eastern European peoples. In order to be prepared to help re-establish historic ties of friendship, I am asking the Congress for increased discretion to use economic tools in this area whenever this is found to be clearly in the national interest. This will require amendment of the Mutual Defense Assistance Control Act along the lines I proposed as a member of the Senate, and upon which the Senate voted last summer. Meanwhile, I hope to explore with the Polish government the possibility of using our frozen Polish funds on projects of peace that will demonstrate our abiding friendship for and interest in the people of Poland.

Third, we must sharpen our political and diplomatic tools - the means of cooperation and agreement on which an enforceable world order must ultimately rest.

I have already taken steps to coordinate and expand our disarmament effort - to increase our programs of research and study - and to make arms control a central goal of our national policy under my direction. The deadly arms race, and the huge resources it absorbs, have too long overshadowed all else we must do. We must prevent that arms race from spreading to new nations, to new nuclear powers and to the reaches of outer space. We must make certain that our negotiators are better informed and better prepared - to formulate workable proposals of our own and to make sound judgments about the proposals of others.

I have asked the other governments concerned to agree to a reasonable delay in the talks on a nuclear test ban -

and it is our intention to resume negotiations prepared to reach a final agreement with any nation that is equally willing to agree to an effective and enforceable treaty.

We must increase our support of the United Nations as an instrument to end the Cold War instead of an arena in which to fight it. In recognition of its increasing importance and the doubling of its membership

- we are enlarging and strengthening our own mission to the U.N.

- we shall help insure that it is properly financed.

- we shall work to see that the integrity of the office of the Secretary-General is maintained.

- And I would address a special plea to the smaller nations of the world - to join with us in strengthening this organization, which is far more essential to their security than it is to ours - the only body in the world where no nation need be powerful to be secure, where every nation has an equal voice, and where any nation can exert influence not according to the strength of its armies but according to the strength of its ideas. It deserves the support of all.

Finally, this Administration intends to explore promptly all possible areas of cooperation with the Soviet Union and other nations "to invoke the wonders of science instead of its terrors." Specifically, I now invite all nations - including the Soviet Union - to join with us in developing a weather prediction program, in a new communications satellite program and in preparation for probing the distant planets of Mars and

Venus, probes which may someday unlock the deepest secrets of the universe.

Today this country is ahead in the science and technology of space, while the Soviet Union is ahead in the capacity to lift large vehicles into orbit. Both nations would help themselves as well as other nations by removing these endeavors from the bitter and wasteful competition of the Cold War. The United States would be willing to join with the Soviet Union and the scientists of all nations in a greater effort to make the fruits of this new knowledge available to all - and, beyond that, in an effort to extend farm technology to hungry nations - to wipe out disease - to increase the exchanges of scientists and their knowledge - and to make our own laboratories available to technicians of other lands who lack the facilities to pursue their own work. Where nature makes natural allies of us all, we can demonstrate that beneficial relations are possible even with those with whom we most deeply disagree - and this must someday be the basis of world peace and world law.

V.

I have commented on the state of the domestic economy, our balance of payments, our Federal and social budget and the state of the world. I would like to conclude with a few remarks about the state of the Executive branch. We have found it full of honest and useful public servants - but their capacity to act decisively at the exact time action is needed has too often been muffled in the morass of committees, timidities and fictitious theories which have created a growing gap between decision and execution, between planning and reality. In a time of rapidly deteriorating situations at home and abroad, this is bad for the public service and particularly bad for the country; and we mean to make a change.

I have pledged myself and my colleagues in the cabinet to a continuous encouragement of initiative, responsibility and energy in serving the public interest. Let every public servant know, whether his post is high or low, that a man's rank and reputation in this Administration will be determined by the size of the job he does, and not by the size of his staff, his office or his budget. Let it be clear that this Administration recognizes the value of dissent and daring - that we greet healthy controversy as the hallmark of healthy change. Let the public service be a proud and lively career. And let every man and woman who works in any area of our national government, in any branch, at any level, be able to say with pride and with honor in future years: "I served the United States government in that hour of our nation's need."

For only with complete dedication by us all to the national interest can we bring our country through the troubled years that lie ahead. Our problems are critical. The tide is unfavorable. The news will be worse before it is better. And while hoping and working for the best, we should prepare ourselves now for the worst.

We cannot escape our dangers - neither must we let them drive us into panic or narrow isolation. In many areas of the world where the balance of power already rests with our adversaries, the forces of freedom are sharply divided. It is one of the ironies of our time that the techniques of a harsh and repressive system should be able to instill discipline and ardor in its servants - while the blessings of liberty have too often stood for privilege, materialism and a life of ease.

But I have a different view of liberty.

Life in 1961 will not be easy. Wishing it, predicting it, even asking for it, will not make it so. There will be further setbacks before the tide is turned. But turn it we must. The hopes of all mankind rest upon us - not simply upon those of us in this chamber, but upon the peasant in Laos, the fisherman in Nigeria, the exile from Cuba, the spirit that moves every man and Nation who shares our hopes for freedom and the future. And in the final analysis, they rest most of all upon the pride and perseverance of our fellow citizens of the great Republic.

In the words of a great President, whose birthday we honor today, closing his final State of the Union Message sixteen years ago, "We pray that we may be worthy of the unlimited opportunities that God has given us."

State of the Union Address
John F. Kennedy
January 11, 1962

Mr. Vice President, my old colleague from Massachusetts and your new Speaker, John McCormack, Members of the 87th Congress, ladies and gentlemen:

This week we begin anew our joint and separate efforts to build the American future. But, sadly, we build without a man who linked a long past with the present and looked strongly to the future. "Mister Sam" Rayburn is gone. Neither this House nor the Nation is the same without him.

Members of the Congress, the Constitution makes us not rivals for power but partners for progress. We are all trustees for the American people, custodians of the American heritage. It is my task to report the State of the Union - to improve it is the task of us all.

In the past year, I have traveled not only across our own land but to other lands - to the North and the South, and across the seas. And I have found - as I am sure you have, in your travels - that people everywhere, in spite of occasional disappointments, look to us - not to our wealth or power, but to the splendor of our ideals. For our Nation is commissioned by history to be either an observer of freedom's failure or the cause of its success. Our overriding obligation in the months ahead is to fulfill the world's hopes by fulfilling our own faith.

I. STRENGTHENING THE ECONOMY

That task must begin at home. For if we cannot fulfill our own ideals here, we cannot expect others to accept them. And when the youngest child alive today has grown to the cares of manhood, our position in the world will be determined first of all by what provisions we make today - for his education, his health, and his opportunities for a good home and a good job and a good life.

At home, we began the year in the valley of recession - we completed it on the high road of recovery and growth. With the help of new Congressionally approved or Administratively increased stimulants to our economy, the number of major surplus labor areas has declined from 101 to 60; non-agricultural employment has increased by more than a million jobs; and the average factory work-week has risen to well over 40 hours. At year's end the economy which Mr. Khrushchev once called a "stumbling horse" was racing to new records in consumer spending, labor income, and industrial production.

We are gratified - but we are not satisfied. Too many unemployed are still looking for the blessings of prosperity. As those who leave our schools and farms demand new jobs, automation takes old jobs away. To expand our growth and job opportunities, I urge on the Congress three measures:

(1) First, the Manpower Training and Development Act, to stop the waste of able-bodied men and women who want to work, but whose only skill has been replaced by a machine, or moved with a mill, or shut down with a mine;

(2) Second, the Youth Employment Opportunities Act, to help train and place not only the one million young Americans who are both out of school and out of work, but the twenty-six million young Americans entering the labor market in this decade; and

(3) Third, the 8 percent tax credit for investment in machinery and equipment, which, combined with planned revisions of depreciation allowances, will spur our modernization, our growth, and our ability to compete abroad.

Moreover - pleasant as it may be to bask in the warmth of recovery - let us not forget that we have suffered three recessions in the last 7 years. The time to repair the roof is when the sun is shining - by filling three basic gaps in our anti-recession protection. We need:

(1) First, Presidential stand-by authority, subject to Congressional veto, to adjust personal income tax rates downward within a specified range and time, to slow down an economic decline before it has dragged us all down;

(2) Second, Presidential stand-by authority, upon a given rise in the rate of unemployment, to accelerate

Federal and Federally-aided capital improvement programs; and

(3) Third, a permanent strengthening of our unemployment compensation system - to maintain for our fellow citizens searching for a job who cannot find it, their purchasing power and their living standards without constant resort - as we have seen in recent years by the Congress and the Administrations - to temporary supplements.

If we enact this six-part program, we can show the whole world that a free economy need not be an unstable economy - that a free system need not leave men unemployed - and that a free society is not only the most productive but the most stable form of organization yet fashioned by man.

II. FIGHTING INFLATION

But recession is only one enemy of a free economy - inflation is another. Last year, 1961, despite rising production and demand, consumer prices held almost steady - and wholesale prices declined. This is the best record of overall price stability of any comparable period of recovery since the end of World War II.

Inflation too often follows in the shadow of growth - while price stability is made easy by stagnation or controls. But we mean to maintain both stability and growth in a climate of freedom.

Our first line of defense against inflation is the good

sense and public spirit of business and labor - keeping their total increases in wages and profits in step with productivity. There is no single statistical test to guide each company and each union. But I strongly urge them - for their country's interest, and for their own - to apply the test of the public interest to these transactions.

Within this same framework of growth and wage-price stability:

- This administration has helped keep our economy competitive by widening the access of small business to credit and Government contracts, and by stepping up the drive against monopoly, price-fixing, and racketeering;

- We will submit a Federal Pay Reform bill aimed at giving our classified, postal, and other employees new pay scales more comparable to those of private industry;

- We are holding the fiscal 1962 budget deficit far below the level incurred after the last recession in 1958; and, finally,

- I am submitting for fiscal 1963 a balanced Federal Budget.

This is a joint responsibility, requiring Congressional cooperation on appropriations, and on three sources of income in particular:

(1) First, an increase in postal rates, to end the postal deficit;

(2) Second, passage of the tax reforms previously urged, to remove unwarranted tax preferences, and to apply to dividends and to interest the same withholding requirements we have long applied to wages; and

(3) Third, extension of the present excise and corporation tax rates, except for those changes - which will be recommended in a message - affecting transportation.

III. GETTING AMERICA MOVING

But a stronger nation and economy require more than a balanced Budget. They require progress in those programs that spur our growth and fortify our strength.

CITIES

A strong America depends on its cities - America's glory, and sometimes America's shame. To substitute sunlight for congestion and progress for decay, we have stepped up existing urban renewal and housing programs, and launched new ones - redoubled the attack on water pollution - speeded aid to airports, hospitals, highways, and our declining mass transit systems - and secured new weapons to combat organized crime, racketeering, and youth delinquency, assisted by the coordinated and hard-hitting efforts of our investigative services: the FBI, the Internal Revenue, the Bureau of Narcotics, and many others. We shall need further anti-crime, mass transit, and transportation legislation - and new tools to fight air pollution. And with all this effort under way, both equity and common sense require that our nation's urban areas - containing three-fourths of our population - sit as equals at the Cabinet table. I urge a new Department of Urban Affairs and Housing.

AGRICULTURE AND RESOURCES

A strong America also depends on its farms and natural resources. American farmers took heart in 1961 - from a billion dollar rise in farm income - and from a hopeful start on reducing the farm surpluses. But we are still operating under a patchwork accumulation of old laws, which cost us $1 billion a year in CCC carrying charges alone, yet fail to halt rural poverty or boost farm earnings.

Our task is to master and turn to fully fruitful ends the magnificent productivity of our farms and farmers. The revolution on our own countryside stands in the sharpest contrast to the repeated farm failures of the Communist nations and is a source of pride to us all. Since 1950 our agricultural output per man-hour has actually doubled! Without new, realistic measures, it will someday swamp our farmers and our taxpayers in a national scandal or a farm depression.

I will, therefore, submit to the Congress a new comprehensive farm program - tailored to fit the use of our land and the supplies of each crop to the long-range needs of the sixties - and designed to prevent chaos in the sixties with a program of common sense.

We also need for the sixties - if we are to bequeath our full national estate to our heirs - a new long-range conservation and recreation program - expansion of our superb National Parks and Forests - preservation of our authentic wilderness areas - new starts on water and power projects as our population steadily increases - and expanded REA generation and transmission loans.

CIVIL RIGHTS

But America stands for progress in human rights as well as economic affairs, and a strong America requires the assurance of full and equal rights to all its citizens, of any race or of any color. This Administration has shown as never before how much could be done through the full use of Executive powers - through the enforcement of laws already passed by the Congress - through persuasion, negotiation, and litigation, to secure the constitutional rights of all: the right to vote, the right to travel without hindrance across State lines, and the right to free public education.

I issued last March a comprehensive order to guarantee the right to equal employment opportunity in all Federal agencies and contractors. The Vice President's Committee thus created has done much, including the voluntary "Plans for Progress" which, in all sections of the country, are achieving a quiet but striking success in opening up to all races new professional, supervisory, and other job opportunities.

But there is much more to be done - by the Executive,

by the courts, and by the Congress. Among the bills now pending before you, on which the Executive Departments will comment in detail, are appropriate methods of strengthening these basic rights which have our full support. The right to vote, for example, should no longer be denied through such arbitrary devices on a local level, sometimes abused, such as literacy tests and poll taxes. As we approach the 100th anniversary, next January, of the Emancipation Proclamation, let the acts of every branch of the Government - and every citizen - portray that "righteousness does exalt a nation."

HEALTH AND WELFARE

Finally, a strong America cannot neglect the aspirations of its citizens - the welfare of the needy, the health care of the elderly, the education of the young. For we are not developing the Nation's wealth for its own sake. Wealth is the means - and people are the ends. All our material riches will avail us little if we do not use them to expand the opportunities of our people. Last year, we improved the diet of needy people - provided more hot lunches and fresh milk to school children - built more college dormitories - and, for the elderly, expanded private housing, nursing homes, health services, and social security. But we have just begun.

To help those least fortunate of all, I am recommending a new public welfare program, stressing services instead of support, rehabilitation instead of relief, and training for useful work instead of prolonged dependency.

To relieve the critical shortage of doctors and dentists - and this is a matter which should concern us all - and expand research, I urge action to aid medical and dental colleges and scholarships and to establish new National Institutes of Health.

To take advantage of modern vaccination achievements, I am proposing a mass immunization program, aimed at the virtual elimination of such ancient enemies of our children as polio, diphtheria, whooping cough, and tetanus.

To protect our consumers from the careless and the unscrupulous, I shall recommend improvements in the Food and Drug laws - strengthening inspection and standards, halting unsafe and worthless products, preventing misleading labels, and cracking down on the illicit sale of habit-forming drugs.

But in matters of health, no piece of unfinished business is more important or more urgent than the enactment under the social security system of health insurance for the aged.

For our older citizens have longer and more frequent illnesses, higher hospital and medical bills and too little income to pay them. Private health insurance helps very few - for its cost is high and its coverage limited. Public welfare cannot help those too proud to seek relief but hard-pressed to pay their own bills. Nor can their children or grandchildren always sacrifice their own health budgets to meet this constant drain.

Social security has long helped to meet the hardships of retirement, death, and disability. I now urge that its coverage be extended without further delay to provide health insurance for the elderly.

EDUCATION

Equally important to our strength is the quality of our education. Eight million adult Americans are classified as functionally illiterate. This is a disturbing figure - reflected in Selective Service rejection rates - reflected in welfare rolls and crime rates. And I shall recommend plans for a massive attack to end this adult illiteracy.

I shall also recommend bills to improve educational quality, to stimulate the arts, and, at the college level, to provide Federal loans for the construction of academic facilities and Federally financed scholarships.

If this Nation is to grow in wisdom and strength, then every able high school graduate should have the opportunity to develop his talents. Yet nearly half lack either the funds or the facilities to attend college. Enrollments are going to double in our colleges in the short space of 10 years. The annual cost per student is skyrocketing to astronomical levels - now averaging $1,650 a year, although almost half of our families earn less than $5,000. They cannot afford such costs - but this Nation cannot afford to maintain its military power and neglect its brainpower.

But excellence in education must begin at the elementary level. I sent to the Congress last year a proposal for Federal aid to public school construction and teachers' salaries. I believe that bill, which passed the Senate and received House Committee approval, offered the minimum amount required by our needs and - in terms of across-the-board aid - the maximum scope permitted by our Constitution. I therefore see no reason to weaken or withdraw that bill, and I urge its passage at this session.

"Civilization," said H. G. Wells, "is a race between education and catastrophe." It is up to you in this Congress to determine the winner of that race.

These are not unrelated measures addressed to specific gaps or grievances in our national life. They are the pattern of our intentions and the foundation of our hopes. "I believe in democracy," said Woodrow Wilson, "because it releases the energy of every human being." The dynamic of democracy is the power and the purpose of the individual, and the policy of this administration is to give to the individual the opportunity to realize his own highest possibilities.

Our program is to open to all the opportunity for steady and productive employment, to remove from all the handicap of arbitrary or irrational exclusion, to offer to all the facilities for education and health and welfare, to make society the servant of the individual and the individual the source of progress, and thus to realize for all the full promise of American life.

IV. OUR GOALS ABROAD

All of these efforts at home give meaning to our efforts abroad. Since the close of the Second World War, a global civil war has divided and tormented mankind. But it is not our military might, or our higher standard of living, that has most distinguished us from our adversaries. It is our belief that the state is the servant of the citizen and not his master.

This basic clash of ideas and wills is but one of the forces reshaping our globe - swept as it is by the tides of hope and fear, by crises in the headlines today that become mere footnotes tomorrow. Both the successes and the setbacks of the past year remain on our agenda of unfinished business. For every apparent blessing contains the seeds of danger - every area of trouble gives out a ray of hope - and the one unchangeable certainty is that nothing is certain or unchangeable.

Yet our basic goal remains the same: a peaceful world community of free and independent states - free to choose their own future and their own system, so long as it does not threaten the freedom of others.

Some may choose forms and ways that we would not choose for ourselves - but it is not for us that they are choosing. We can welcome diversity - the Communists cannot. For we offer a world of choice - they offer the world of coercion. And the way of the past shows clearly that freedom, not coercion, is the wave of the future. At times our goal has been obscured by crisis or endangered by conflict - but it draws sustenance from five basic sources of strength:

- the moral and physical strength of the United States;

- the united strength of the Atlantic Community;

- the regional strength of our Hemispheric relations;

John F. Kennedy

- the creative strength of our efforts in the new and developing nations; and

- the peace-keeping strength of the United Nations.

V. OUR MILITARY STRENGTH

Our moral and physical strength begins at home as already discussed. But it includes our military strength as well. So long as fanaticism and fear brood over the affairs of men, we must arm to deter others from aggression.

In the past 12 months our military posture has steadily improved. We increased the previous defense budget by 15 percent - not in the expectation of war but for the preservation of peace. We more than doubled our acquisition rate of Polaris submarines - we doubled the production capacity for Minuteman missiles - and increased by 50 percent the number of manned bombers standing ready on a 15 minute alert. This year the combined force levels planned under our new Defense budget - including nearly three hundred additional Polaris and Minuteman missiles - have been precisely calculated to insure the continuing strength of our nuclear deterrent.

But our strength may be tested at many levels. We intend to have at all times the capacity to resist non-nuclear or limited attacks - as a complement to our nuclear capacity, not as a substitute. We have rejected any all-or-nothing posture which would leave no choice but inglorious retreat or unlimited retaliation.

Thus we have doubled the number of ready combat divisions in the Army's strategic reserve - increased our troops in Europe - built up the Marines - added new sealift and airlift capacity - modernized our weapons and ammunition - expanded our anti-guerrilla forces - and increased the active fleet by more than 70 vessels and our tactical air forces by nearly a dozen wings.

Because we needed to reach this higher long-term level of readiness more quickly, 155,000 members of the Reserve and National Guard were activated under the Act of this Congress. Some disruptions and distress were inevitable. But the overwhelming majority bear their burdens - and their Nation's burdens - with admirable and traditional devotion.

In the coming year, our reserve programs will be revised - two Army Divisions will, I hope, replace those Guard Divisions on duty - and substantial other increases will boost our Air Force fighter units, the procurement of equipment, and our continental defense and warning efforts. The Nation's first serious civil defense shelter program is under way, identifying, marking, and stocking 50 million spaces; and I urge your approval of Federal incentives for the construction of public fall-out shelters in schools and hospitals and similar centers.

VI. THE UNITED NATIONS

But arms alone are not enough to keep the peace - it must be kept by men. Our instrument and our hope is the United Nations - and I see little merit in the impatience of those who would abandon this imperfect world instrument because they dislike our imperfect world. For the troubles of a world organization merely reflect the troubles of the world itself. And if the organization is weakened, these troubles can only increase. We may not always agree with every detailed action taken by every officer of the United Nations, or with every voting majority. But as an institution, it should have in the future, as it has had in the past since its inception, no stronger or more faithful member than the United States of America.

In 1961 the peace-keeping strength of the United Nations was reinforced. And those who preferred or predicted its demise, envisioning a troika in the seat of Hammarskjold - or Red China inside the Assembly - have seen instead a new vigor, under a new Secretary General and a fully independent Secretariat. In making plans for a new forum and principles on disarmament - for peace-keeping in outer space - for a decade of development effort - the UN fulfilled its Charter's lofty aim.

Eighteen months ago the tangled and turbulent Congo presented the UN with its gravest challenge. The prospect was one of chaos - or certain big-power confrontation, with all of its hazards and all of its risks, to us and to others. Today the hopes have improved for peaceful conciliation within a united Congo. This is the objective of our policy in this important area.

No policeman is universally popular - particularly when he uses his stick to restore law and order on his beat. Those members who are willing to contribute their votes and their views - but very little else - have created a serious deficit by refusing to pay their share of special UN assessments. Yet they do pay their annual assessments to retain their votes - and a new UN Bond issue, financing special operations for the next 18 months, is to be repaid with interest from these regular assessments. This is clearly in our interest. It will not only keep the UN solvent, but require all voting members to pay their fair share of its activities. Our share of special operations has long been much higher than our share of the annual assessment - and the bond issue will in effect reduce our disproportionate obligation, and for these reasons, I am urging Congress to approve our participation.

With the approval of this Congress, we have undertaken in the past year a great new effort in outer space. Our aim is not simply to be first on the moon, any more than Charles Lindbergh's real aim was to be the first to Paris. His aim was to develop the techniques of our own country and other countries in the field of air and the atmosphere, and our objective in making this effort, which we hope will place one of our citizens on the moon, is to develop in a new frontier of science, commerce and cooperation, the position of the United States and the Free World.

This Nation belongs among the first to explore it, and among the first - if not the first - we shall be. We are offering our know-how and our cooperation to the United Nations. Our satellites will soon be providing other nations with improved weather observations. And I shall soon send to the Congress a measure to govern the financing and operation of an International Communications Satellite system, in a manner consistent with the public interest and our foreign policy.

John F. Kennedy

But peace in space will help us naught once peace on earth is gone. World order will be secured only when the whole world has laid down these weapons which seem to offer us present security but threaten the future survival of the human race. That armistice day seems very far away. The vast resources of this planet are being devoted more and more to the means of destroying, instead of enriching, human life.

But the world was not meant to be a prison in which man awaits his execution. Nor has mankind survived the tests and trials of thousands of years to surrender everything - including its existence - now. This Nation has the will and the faith to make a supreme effort to break the log jam on disarmament and nuclear tests - and we will persist until we prevail, until the rule of law has replaced the ever dangerous use of force.

VII. LATIN AMERICA

I turn now to a prospect of great promise: our Hemispheric relations. The Alliance for Progress is being rapidly transformed from proposal to program. Last month in Latin America I saw for myself the quickening of hope, the revival of confidence, the new trust in our country - among workers and farmers as well as diplomats. We have pledged our help in speeding their economic, educational, and social progress. The Latin American Republics have in turn pledged a new and strenuous effort of self-help and self-reform.

To support this historic undertaking, I am proposing -

under the authority contained in the bills of the last session of the Congress - a special long-term Alliance for Progress fund of $3 billion. Combined with our Food for Peace, Export-Import Bank, and other resources, this will provide more than $1 billion a year in new support for the Alliance. In addition, we have increased twelve-fold our Spanish and Portuguese language broadcasting in Latin America, and improved Hemispheric trade and defense. And while the blight of communism has been increasingly exposed and isolated in the Americas, liberty has scored a gain. The people of the Dominican Republic, with our firm encouragement and help, and those of our sister Republics of this Hemisphere, are safely passing through the treacherous course from dictatorship through disorder towards democracy.

VIII. THE NEW AND DEVELOPING NATIONS

Our efforts to help other new or developing nations, and to strengthen their stand for freedom, have also made progress. A newly unified Agency for International Development is reorienting our foreign assistance to emphasize long-term development loans instead of grants, more economic aid instead of military, individual plans to meet the individual needs of the nations, and new standards on what they must do to marshal their own resources.

A newly conceived Peace Corps is winning friends and helping people in fourteen countries - supplying trained and dedicated young men and women, to give these new nations a hand in building a society, and a glimpse of the best that is in our country. If there is a problem here, it is that we cannot supply the spontaneous and mounting demand.

A newly-expanded Food for Peace Program is feeding the hungry of many lands with the abundance of our productive farms - providing lunches for children in school, wages for economic development, relief for the victims of flood and famine, and a better diet for millions whose daily bread is their chief concern.

These programs help people; and, by helping people, they help freedom. The views of their governments may sometimes be very different from ours - but events in Africa, the Middle East, and Eastern Europe teach us never to write off any nation as lost to the Communists. That is the lesson of our time. We support the independence of those newer or weaker states whose history, geography, economy or lack of power impels them to remain outside "entangling alliances" - as we did for more than a century. For the independence of nations is a bar to the Communists' "grand design" - it is the basis of our own.

In the past year, for example, we have urged a neutral and independent Laos - regained there a common policy with our major allies - and insisted that a cease-fire precede negotiations. While a workable formula for supervising its independence is still to be achieved, both the spread of war - which might have involved this country also - and a Communist occupation have thus far been prevented.

A satisfactory settlement in Laos would also help to achieve and safeguard the peace in Viet-Nam - where the foe is increasing his tactics of terror - where our own efforts have been stepped up - and where the local government has initiated new programs and reforms to broaden the base of resistance. The systematic aggression now bleeding that country is not a "war of liberation" - for Viet-Nam is already free. It is a war of attempted subjugation - and it will be resisted.

IX. THE ATLANTIC COMMUNITY

Finally, the united strength of the Atlantic Community has flourished in the last year under severe tests. NATO has increased both the number and the readiness of its air, ground, and naval units - both its nuclear and non-nuclear capabilities. Even greater efforts by all its members are still required. Nevertheless our unity of purpose and will has been, I believe, immeasurably strengthened.

The threat to the brave city of Berlin remains. In these last 6 months the Allies have made it unmistakably clear that our presence in Berlin, our free access thereto, and the freedom of two million West Berliners would not be surrendered either to force or through appeasement - and to maintain those rights and obligations, we are prepared to talk, when appropriate, and to fight, if necessary. Every member of NATO stands with us in a common commitment to preserve this symbol of free man's will to remain free.

I cannot now predict the course of future negotiations over Berlin. I can only say that we are sparing no honorable effort to find a peaceful and mutually acceptable resolution of this problem. I believe such a resolution can be found, and with it an improvement in our relations with the Soviet Union, if only the leaders in the Kremlin will recognize the basic rights and interests involved, and the interest of all mankind in peace.

But the Atlantic Community is no longer concerned with purely military aims. As its common undertakings grow at an ever-increasing pace, we are, and increasingly will be, partners in aid, trade, defense, diplomacy, and monetary affairs.

The emergence of the new Europe is being matched by the emergence of new ties across the Atlantic. It is a matter of undramatic daily cooperation in hundreds of workaday tasks: of currencies kept in effective relation, of development loans meshed together, of standardized weapons, and concerted diplomatic positions. The Atlantic Community grows, not like a volcanic mountain, by one mighty explosion, but like a coral reef, from the accumulating activity of all.

Thus, we in the free world are moving steadily toward unity and cooperation, in the teeth of that old Bolshevik prophecy, and at the very time when extraordinary rumbles of discord can be heard across the Iron Curtain. It is not free societies which bear within them the seeds of inevitable disunity.

X. OUR BALANCE OF PAYMENTS

On one special problem, of great concern to our friends, and to us, I am proud to give the Congress an encouraging report. Our efforts to safeguard the dollar are progressing. In the 11 months preceding last February 1, we suffered a net loss of nearly $2 billion in gold. In the 11 months that followed, the loss was just over half a billion dollars. And our deficit in our basic transactions with the rest of the world - trade, defense, foreign aid, and capital, excluding volatile short-term flows - has been reduced from $2 billion for 1960 to about one-third that amount for 1961. Speculative fever against the dollar is ending - and confidence in the dollar has been restored.

We did not - and could not - achieve these gains through import restrictions, troop withdrawals, exchange controls, dollar devaluation or choking off domestic recovery. We acted not in panic but in perspective. But the problem is not yet solved. Persistently large deficits would endanger our economic growth and our military and defense commitments abroad. Our goal must be a reasonable equilibrium in our balance of payments. With the cooperation of the Congress, business, labor, and our major allies, that goal can be reached.

We shall continue to attract foreign tourists and investments to our shores, to seek increased military purchases here by our allies, to maximize foreign aid procurement from American firms, to urge increased aid from other fortunate nations to the less fortunate, to seek tax laws which do not favor investment in other industrialized nations or tax havens, and to urge coordination of allied fiscal and monetary policies so as to discourage large and disturbing capital movements.

TRADE

Above all, if we are to pay for our commitments abroad, we must expand our exports. Our businessmen must be export conscious and export competitive. Our tax policies must spur modernization of our plants - our wage and price gains must be consistent with productivity to hold the line on prices - our export credit and promotion campaigns for American industries must continue to expand.

But the greatest challenge of all is posed by the growth of the European Common Market. Assuming the accession of the United Kingdom, there will arise across the Atlantic a trading partner behind a single external tariff similar to ours with an economy which nearly equals our own. Will we in this country adapt our thinking to these new prospects and patterns - or will we wait until events have passed us by?

This is the year to decide. The Reciprocal Trade Act is expiring. We need a new law - a wholly new approach - a bold new instrument of American trade policy. Our decision could well affect the unity of the West, the course of the Cold War, and the economic growth of our Nation for a generation to come.

If we move decisively, our factories and farms can increase their sales to their richest, fastest-growing market. Our exports will increase. Our balance of payments position will improve. And we will have forged across the Atlantic a trading partnership with vast resources for freedom.

If, on the other hand, we hang back in deference to

local economic pressures, we will find ourselves cut off from our major allies. Industries - and I believe this is most vital - industries will move their plants and jobs and capital inside the walls of the Common Market, and jobs, therefore, will be lost here in the United States if they cannot otherwise compete for its consumers. Our farm surpluses - our balance of trade, as you all know, to Europe, the Common Market, in farm products, is nearly three or four to one in our favor, amounting to one of the best earners of dollars in our balance of payments structure, and without entrance to this Market, without the ability to enter it, our farm surpluses will pile up in the Middle West, tobacco in the South, and other commodities, which have gone through Western Europe for 15 years. Our balance of payments position will worsen. Our consumers will lack a wider choice of goods at lower prices. And millions of American workers - whose jobs depend on the sale or the transportation or the distribution of exports or imports, or whose jobs will be endangered by the movement of our capital to Europe, or whose jobs can be maintained only in an expanding economy - these millions of workers in your home States and mine will see their real interests sacrificed.

Members of the Congress: The United States did not rise to greatness by waiting for others to lead. This Nation is the world's foremost manufacturer, farmer, banker, consumer, and exporter. The Common Market is moving ahead at an economic growth rate twice ours. The Communist economic offensive is under way. The opportunity is ours - the initiative is up to us - and I believe that 1962 is the time.

To seize that initiative, I shall shortly send to the

Congress a new five-year Trade Expansion Action, far-reaching in scope but designed with great care to make certain that its benefits to our people far outweigh any risks. The bill will permit the gradual elimination of tariffs here in the United States and in the Common Market on those items in which we together supply 80 percent of the world's trade - mostly items in which our own ability to compete is demonstrated by the fact that we sell abroad, in these items, substantially more than we import. This step will make it possible for our major industries to compete with their counterparts in Western Europe for access to European consumers.

On other goods the bill will permit a gradual reduction of duties up to 50 percent - permitting bargaining by major categories - and provide for appropriate and tested forms of assistance to firms and employees adjusting to import competition. We are not neglecting the safeguards provided by peril points, an escape clause, or the National Security Amendment. Nor are we abandoning our non-European friends or our traditional "most-favored nation" principle. On the contrary, the bill will provide new encouragement for their sale of tropical agricultural products, so important to our friends in Latin America, who have long depended upon the European market, who now find themselves faced with new challenges which we must join with them in overcoming.

Concessions, in this bargaining, must of course be reciprocal, not unilateral. The Common Market will not fulfill its own high promise unless its outside tariff walls are low. The dangers of restriction or timidity in our own policy have counterparts for our friends in Europe. For together we face a common challenge: to enlarge the prosperity of free men everywhere - to build in partnership a new trading community in which all free nations may gain from the productive energy of free competitive effort.

These various elements in our foreign policy lead, as I have said, to a single goal - the goal of a peaceful world of free and independent states. This is our guide for the present and our vision for the future - a free community of nations, independent but interdependent, uniting north and south, east and west, in one great family of man, outgrowing and transcending the hates and fears that rend our age.

We will not reach that goal today, or tomorrow. We may not reach it in our own lifetime. But the quest is the greatest adventure of our century. We sometimes chafe at the burden of our obligations, the complexity of our decisions, the agony of our choices. But there is no comfort or security for us in evasion, no solution in abdication, no relief in irresponsibility.

A year ago, in assuming the tasks of the Presidency, I said that few generations, in all history, had been granted the role of being the great defender of freedom in its hour of maximum danger. This is our good fortune, and I welcome it now as I did a year ago. For it is the fate of this generation - of you in the Congress and of me as President - to live with a struggle we did not start, in a world we did not make. But the pressures of life are not always distributed by choice. And while no nation has ever faced such a challenge, no nation has ever been so ready to seize the burden and the glory of freedom.

And in this high endeavor, may God watch over the United States of America.

State of the Union Address
John F. Kennedy
January 14, 1963

Mr. Vice President, Mr. Speaker, Members of the 88th Congress:

I congratulate you all - not merely on your electoral victory but on your selected role in history. For you and I are privileged to serve the great Republic in what could be the most decisive decade in its long history. The choices we make, for good or ill, may well shape the state of the Union for generations yet to come.

Little more than 100 weeks ago I assumed the office of President of the United States. In seeking the help of the Congress and our countrymen, I pledged no easy answers. I pledged - and asked - only toil and dedication. These the Congress and the people have given in good measure. And today, having witnessed in recent months a heightened respect for our national purpose and power - having seen the courageous calm of a united people in a perilous hour - and having observed a steady improvement in the opportunities and well-being of our citizens - I can report to you that the state of this old but youthful Union, in the 175th year of its life, is good.

In the world beyond our borders, steady progress has been made in building a world of order. The people of West Berlin remain both free and secure. A settlement, though still precarious, has been reached in Laos. The spearpoint of aggression has been blunted in Viet-Nam. The end of agony may be in sight in the Congo. The doctrine of troika is dead. And, while danger continues, a deadly threat has been removed in Cuba.

At home, the recession is behind us. Well over a million more men and women are working today than were working 2 years ago. The average factory work week is once again more than 40 hours; our industries are turning out more goods than ever before; and more than half of the manufacturing capacity that lay silent and wasted 100 weeks ago is humming with activity.

In short, both at home and abroad, there may now be a temptation to relax. For the road has been long, the burden heavy, and the pace consistently urgent.

But we cannot be satisfied to rest here. This is the side of the hill, not the top. The mere absence of war is not peace. The mere absence of recession is not growth. We have made a beginning - but we have only begun.

Now the time has come to make the most of our gains - to translate the renewal of our national strength into the achievement of our national purpose.

I.

America has enjoyed 22 months of uninterrupted economic recovery. But recovery is not enough. If we are to prevail in the long run, we must expand the long-run strength of our economy. We must move along the path to a higher rate of growth and full employment.

For this would mean tens of billions of dollars more each year in production, profits, wages, and public revenues. It would mean an end to the persistent slack which has kept our unemployment at or above 5 percent for 61 out of the past 62 months - and an end to the growing pressures for such restrictive measures as the 35-hour week, which alone could increase hourly labor costs by as much as 14 percent, start a new wage-price spiral of inflation, and undercut our efforts to compete with other nations.

To achieve these greater gains, one step, above all, is essential - the enactment this year of a substantial reduction and revision in Federal income taxes.

For it is increasingly clear - to those in Government, business, and labor who are responsible for our economy's success - that our obsolete tax system exerts too heavy a drag on private purchasing power, profits, and employment. Designed to check inflation in earlier years, it now checks growth instead. It discourages extra effort and risk. It distorts the use of resources. It invites recurrent recessions, depresses our Federal revenues, and causes chronic budget deficits.

Now, when the inflationary pressures of the war and the post-war years no longer threaten, and the dollar commands new respect - now, when no military crisis strains our resources - now is the time to act. We cannot afford to be timid or slow. For this is the most urgent task confronting the Congress in 1963.

In an early message, I shall propose a permanent reduction in tax rates which will lower liabilities by $13.5 billion. Of this, $11 billion results from reducing individual tax rates, which now range between 20 and 91 percent, to a more sensible range of 14 to 65 percent, with a split in the present first bracket. Two and one-half billion dollars results from reducing corporate tax rates, from 52 percent - which gives the Government today a majority interest in profits - to the permanent pre-Korean level of 47 percent. This is in addition to the more than $2 billion cut in corporate tax liabilities resulting from last year's investment credit and depreciation reform.

To achieve this reduction within the limits of a manageable budgetary deficit, I urge: first, that these cuts be phased over 3 calendar years, beginning in 1963 with a cut of some $6 billion at annual rates; second, that these reductions be coupled with selected structural changes, beginning in 1964, which will broaden the tax base, end unfair or unnecessary preferences, remove or lighten certain hardships, and in the net offset some $3.5 billion of the revenue loss; and third, that budgetary receipts at the outset be increased by $1.5 billion a year, without any change in tax liabilities, by gradually shifting the tax payments of large corporations to a more current time schedule. This combined program, by increasing the amount of our national income, will in time result in still higher Federal revenues. It is a fiscally responsible program - the surest and the soundest way of achieving in time a balanced budget in a balanced full employment economy.

This net reduction in tax liabilities of $10 billion will increase the purchasing power of American families

John F. Kennedy

and business enterprises in every tax bracket, with greatest increase going to our low-income consumers. It will, in addition, encourage the initiative and risk-taking on which our free system depends - induce more investment, production, and capacity use - help provide the 2 million new jobs we need every year - and reinforce the American principle of additional reward for additional effort.

I do not say that a measure for tax reduction and reform is the only way to achieve these goals.

No doubt a massive increase in Federal spending could also create jobs and growth, but in today's setting, private consumers, employers, and investors should be given a full opportunity first.

No doubt a temporary tax cut could provide a spur to our economy - but a long-run problem compels a long-run solution.

No doubt a reduction in either individual or corporation taxes alone would be of great help - but corporations need customers and job seekers need jobs. No doubt tax reduction without reform would sound simpler and more attractive to many - but our growth is also hampered by a host of tax inequities and special preferences which have distorted the flow of investment.

And finally, there are no doubt some who would prefer to put off a tax cut in the hope that ultimately an end to the cold war would make possible an equivalent cut in expenditures - but that end is not in view and to wait for it would be costly and self-defeating.

In submitting a tax program which will, of course, temporarily increase the deficit but can ultimately end it - and in recognition of the need to control expenditures - I will shortly submit a fiscal 1964 administrative budget which, while allowing for needed rises in defense, space, and fixed interest charges, holds total expenditures for all other purposes below this year's level.

This requires the reduction or postponement of many desirable programs, the absorption of a large part of last year's Federal pay raise through personnel and other economies, the termination of certain installations and projects, and the substitution in several programs of private for public credit. But I am convinced that the enactment this year of tax reduction and tax reform overshadows all other domestic problems in this Congress. For we cannot for long lead the cause of peace and freedom, if we ever cease to set the pace here at home.

II.

Tax reduction alone, however, is not enough to strengthen our society, to provide opportunities for the four million Americans who are born every year, to improve the lives of 32 million Americans who live on the outskirts of poverty.

The quality of American life must keep pace with the quantity of American goods.

This country cannot afford to be materially rich and

spiritually poor.

Therefore, by holding down the budgetary cost of existing programs to keep within the limitations I have set, it is both possible and imperative to adopt other new measures that we cannot afford to postpone.

These measures are based on a series of fundamental premises, grouped under four related headings:

First, we need to strengthen our Nation by investing in our youth.

The future of any country which is dependent upon the will and wisdom of its citizens is damaged, and irreparably damaged, whenever any of its children is not educated to the full extent of his talent, from grade school through graduate school. Today, an estimated 4 out of every 10 students in the 5th grade will not even finish high school - and that is a waste we cannot afford.

In addition, there is no reason why one million young Americans, out of school and out of work, should all remain unwanted and often untrained on our city streets when their energies can be put to good use.

Finally, the overseas success of our Peace Corps volunteers, most of them young men and women carrying skills and ideas to needy people, suggests the merit of a similar corps serving our own community needs: in mental hospitals, on Indian reservations, in centers for the aged or for young delinquents, in schools for the illiterate or the handicapped. As the idealism of our youth has served world peace, so can it serve the domestic tranquility.

Second, we need to strengthen our Nation by safeguarding its health.

Our working men and women, instead of being forced to beg for help from public charity once they are old and ill, should start contributing now to their own retirement health program through the Social Security System.

Moreover, all our miracles of medical research will count for little if we cannot reverse the growing nationwide shortage of doctors, dentists, and nurses, and the widespread shortages of nursing homes and modern urban hospital facilities. Merely to keep the present ratio of doctors and dentists from declining any further, we must over the next 10 years increase the capacity of our medical schools by 50 percent and our dental schools by 100 percent.

Finally, and of deep concern, I believe that the abandonment of the mentally ill and the mentally retarded to the grim mercy of custodial institutions too often inflicts on them and on their families a needless cruelty which this Nation should not endure. The incidence of mental retardation in this country is three times as high as that of Sweden, for example - and that figure can and must be reduced.

Third, we need to strengthen our Nation by protecting the basic rights of its citizens.

The right to competent counsel must be assured to every man accused of crime in Federal court, regardless of his means.

And the most precious and powerful right in the world,

the right to vote in a free American election, must not be denied to any citizen on grounds of his race or color. I wish that all qualified Americans permitted to vote were willing to vote, but surely in this centennial year of Emancipation all those who are willing to vote should always be permitted.

Fourth, we need to strengthen our Nation by making the best and the most economical use of its resources and facilities.

Our economic health depends on healthy transportation arteries; and I believe the way to a more modern, economical choice of national transportation service is through increased competition and decreased regulation. Local mass transit, faring even worse, is as essential a community service as hospitals and highways. Nearly three-fourths of our citizens live in urban areas, which occupy only 2 percent of our land - and if local transit is to survive and relieve the congestion of these cities, it needs Federal stimulation and assistance.

Next, this Government is in the storage and stockpile business to the melancholy tune of more than $16 billion. We must continue to support farm income, but we should not pile more farm surpluses on top of the $7.5 billion we already own. We must maintain a stockpile of strategic materials, but the $8.5 billion we have acquired - for reasons both good and bad - is much more than we need; and we should be empowered to dispose of the excess in ways which will not cause market disruption.

Finally, our already overcrowded national parks and recreation areas will have twice as many visitors 10 years from now as they do today. If we do not plan today for the future growth of these and other great natural assets - not only parks and forests but wildlife and wilderness preserves, and water projects of all kinds - our children and their children will be poorer in every sense of the word.

These are not domestic concerns alone. For upon our achievement of greater vitality and strength here at home hang our fate and future in the world: our ability to sustain and supply the security of free men and nations, our ability to command their respect for our leadership, our ability to expand our trade without threat to our balance of payments, and our ability to adjust to the changing demands of cold war competition and challenge.

We shall be judged more by what we do at home than by what we preach abroad. Nothing we could do to help the developing countries would help them half as much as a booming U.S. economy. And nothing our opponents could do to encourage their own ambitions would encourage them half as much as a chronic, lagging U.S. economy. These domestic tasks do not divert energy from our security - they provide the very foundation for freedom's survival and success.

III.

Turning to the world outside, it was only a few years ago - in Southeast Asia, Africa, Eastern Europe, Latin America, even outer space - that communism sought to convey the image of a unified, confident, and expanding empire, closing in on a sluggish America and a free world in disarray. But few people would hold to that picture today.

In these past months we have reaffirmed the scientific and military superiority of freedom. We have doubled our efforts in space, to assure us of being first in the future. We have undertaken the most far-reaching defense improvements in the peacetime history of this country. And we have maintained the frontiers of freedom from Viet-Nam to West Berlin.

But complacency or self-congratulation can imperil our security as much as the weapons of tyranny. A moment of pause is not a promise of peace. Dangerous problems remain from Cuba to the South China Sea. The world's prognosis prescribes, in short, not a year's vacation for us, but a year of obligation and opportunity.

Four special avenues of opportunity stand out: the Atlantic Alliance, the developing nations, the new Sino-Soviet difficulties, and the search for worldwide peace.

IV.

First, how fares the grand alliance? Free Europe is entering into a new phase of its long and brilliant history. The era of colonial expansion has passed; the era of national rivalries is fading; and a new era of interdependence and unity is taking shape. Defying the old prophecies of Marx, consenting to what no conqueror could ever compel, the free nations of Europe are moving toward a unity of purpose and power and policy in every sphere of activity.

For 17 years this movement has had our consistent support, both political and economic. Far from resenting the new Europe, we regard her as a welcome partner, not a rival. For the road to world peace and freedom is still long, and there are burdens which only full partners can share - in supporting the common defense, in expanding world trade, in aligning our balance of payments, in aiding the emergent nations, in concerting political and economic policies, and in welcoming to our common effort other industrialized nations, notably Japan, whose remarkable economic and political development of the 1950's permits it now to play on the world scene a major constructive role.

No doubt differences of opinion will continue to get more attention than agreements on action, as Europe moves from independence to more formal interdependence. But these are honest differences among honorable associates - more real and frequent, in fact, among our Western European allies than between them and the United States. For the unity of freedom has never relied on uniformity of opinion. But the basic agreement of this alliance on fundamental issues continues.

The first task of the alliance remains the common defense. Last month Prime Minister Macmillan and I laid plans for a new stage in our long cooperative effort, one which aims to assist in the wider task of framing a common nuclear defense for the whole alliance.

The Nassau agreement recognizes that the security of the West is indivisible, and so must be our defense. But it also recognizes that this is an alliance of proud and sovereign nations, and works best when we do not forget it. It recognizes further that the nuclear defense of the West is not a matter for the present nuclear powers alone - that France will be such a power in the future - and that ways must be found without increasing the hazards of nuclear diffusion, to increase the role of our other partners in planning, manning, and directing a truly multilateral nuclear force within an increasingly intimate NATO alliance. Finally, the Nassau agreement recognizes that nuclear defense is not enough, that the agreed NATO levels of conventional strength must be met, and that the alliance cannot afford to be in a position of having to answer every threat with nuclear weapons or nothing.

We remain too near the Nassau decisions, and too far from their full realization, to know their place in history. But I believe that, for the first time, the door is open for the nuclear defense of the alliance to become a source of confidence, instead of a cause of contention.

The next most pressing concern of the alliance is our common economic goals of trade and growth. This Nation continues to be concerned about its balance-of-payments deficit, which, despite its decline, remains a stubborn and troublesome problem. We believe, moreover, that closer economic ties among all free nations are essential to prosperity and peace. And neither we nor the members of the European Common Market are so affluent that we can long afford to shelter high cost farms or factories from the winds of foreign competition, or to restrict the channels of trade with other nations of the free world. If the Common Market should move toward protectionism and restrictionism, it would undermine its own basic principles. This Government means to use the authority conferred on it last year by the Congress to encourage trade expansion on both sides of the Atlantic and around the world.

V.

Second, what of the developing and non-aligned nations? They were shocked by the Soviets' sudden and secret attempt to transform Cuba into a nuclear striking base - and by Communist China's arrogant invasion of India. They have been reassured by our prompt assistance to India, by our support through the United Nations of the Congo's unification, by our patient search for disarmament, and by the improvement in our treatment of citizens and visitors whose skins do not happen to be white. And as the older colonialism recedes, and the neo-colonialism of the Communist powers stands out more starkly than ever, they realize more clearly that the issue in the world struggle is not communism versus capitalism, but coercion versus free choice.

They are beginning to realize that the longing for independence is the same the world over, whether it is the independence of West Berlin or Viet-Nam. They are beginning to realize that such independence runs athwart all Communist ambitions but is in keeping with our own - and that our approach to their diverse needs is resilient and resourceful, while the

Communists are still relying on ancient doctrines and dogmas.

Nevertheless it is hard for any nation to focus on an external or subversive threat to its independence when its energies are drained in daily combat with the forces of poverty and despair. It makes little sense for us to assail, in speeches and resolutions, the horrors of communism, to spend $50 billion a year to prevent its military advance - and then to begrudge spending, largely on American products, less than one-tenth of that amount to help other nations strengthen their independence and cure the social chaos in which communism has always thrived.

I am proud - and I think most Americans are proud - of a mutual defense and assistance program, evolved with bipartisan support in three administrations, which has, with all its recognized problems, contributed to the fact that not a single one of the nearly fifty U.N. members to gain independence since the Second World War has succumbed to Communist control.

I am proud of a program that has helped to arm and feed and clothe millions of people who live on the front lines of freedom.

I am especially proud that this country has put forward for the 60's a vast cooperative effort to achieve economic growth and social progress throughout the Americas - the Alliance for Progress.

I do not underestimate the difficulties that we face in this mutual effort among our close neighbors, but the free states of this hemisphere, working in close collaboration, have begun to make this alliance a living reality. Today it is feeding one out of every four school age children in Latin America an extra food ration from our farm surplus. It has distributed 1.5 million school books and is building 17,000 classrooms. It has helped resettle tens of thousands of farm families on land they can call their own. It is stimulating our good neighbors to more self-help and self-reform - fiscal, social, institutional, and land reforms. It is bringing new housing and hope, new health and dignity, to millions who were forgotten. The men and women of this hemisphere know that the alliance cannot succeed if it is only another name for United States handouts - that it can succeed only as the Latin American nations themselves devote their best effort to fulfilling its goals.

This story is the same in Africa, in the Middle East, and in Asia. Wherever nations are willing to help themselves, we stand ready to help them build new bulwarks of freedom. We are not purchasing votes for the cold war; we have gone to the aid of imperiled nations, neutrals and allies alike. What we do ask - and all that we ask - is that our help be used to best advantage, and that their own efforts not be diverted by needless quarrels with other independent nations.

Despite all its past achievements, the continued progress of the Mutual Assistance Program requires a persistent discontent with present performance. We have been reorganizing this program to make it a more effective, efficient instrument - and that process will continue this year.

But free world development will still be an uphill struggle. Government aid can only supplement the role of private investment, trade expansion, commodity stabilization, and, above all, internal self-improvement. The processes of growth are gradual - bearing fruit in a decade, not a day. Our successes will be neither quick nor dramatic. But if these programs were ever to be ended, our failures in a dozen countries would be sudden and certain.

Neither money nor technical assistance, however, can be our only weapon against poverty. In the end, the crucial effort is one of purpose, requiring the fuel of finance but also a torch of idealism. And nothing carries the spirit of this American idealism more effectively to the far corners of the earth than the American Peace Corps.

A year ago, less than 900 Peace Corps volunteers were on the job. A year from now they will number more than 9,000 - men and women, aged 18 to 79, willing to give 2 years of their lives to helping people in other lands.

There are, in fact, nearly a million Americans serving their country and the cause of freedom in overseas posts, a record no other people can match. Surely those of us who stay at home should be glad to help indirectly; by supporting our aid programs; by opening our doors to foreign visitors and diplomats and students; and by proving, day by day, by deed as well as word, that we are a just and generous people.

VI.

Third, what comfort can we take from the increasing

strains and tensions within the Communist bloc? Here hope must be tempered with caution. For the Soviet-Chinese disagreement is over means, not ends. A dispute over how best to bury the free world is no grounds for Western rejoicing.

Nevertheless, while a strain is not a fracture, it is clear that the forces of diversity are at work inside the Communist camp, despite all the iron disciplines of regimentation and all the iron dogmatisms of ideology. Marx is proven wrong once again: for it is the closed Communist societies, not the free and open societies which carry within themselves the seeds of internal disintegration.

The disarray of the Communist empire has been heightened by two other formidable forces. One is the historical force of nationalism - and the yearning of all men to be free. The other is the gross inefficiency of their economies. For a closed society is not open to ideas of progress - and a police state finds that it cannot command the grain to grow.

New nations asked to choose between two competing systems need only compare conditions in East and West Germany, Eastern and Western Europe, North and South Viet-Nam. They need only compare the disillusionment of Communist Cuba with the promise of the Alliance for Progress. And all the world knows that no successful system builds a wall to keep its people in and freedom out - and the wall of shame dividing Berlin is a symbol of Communist failure.

John F. Kennedy

VII.

Finally, what can we do to move from the present pause toward enduring peace? Again I would counsel caution. I foresee no spectacular reversal in Communist methods or goals. But if all these trends and developments can persuade the Soviet Union to walk the path of peace, then let her know that all free nations will journey with her. But until that choice is made, and until the world can develop a reliable system of international security, the free peoples have no choice but to keep their arms nearby.

This country, therefore, continues to require the best defense in the world - a defense which is suited to the sixties. This means, unfortunately, a rising defense budget - for there is no substitute for adequate defense, and no "bargain basement" way of achieving it. It means the expenditure of more than $15 billion this year on nuclear weapons systems alone, a sum which is about equal to the combined defense budgets of our European Allies.

But it also means improved air and missile defenses, improved civil defense, a strengthened anti-guerrilla capacity and, of prime importance, more powerful and flexible non-nuclear forces. For threats of massive retaliation may not deter piecemeal aggression - and a line of destroyers in a quarantine, or a division of well-equipped men on a border, may be more useful to our real security than the multiplication of awesome weapons beyond all rational need.

But our commitment to national safety is not a commitment to expand our military establishment indefinitely. We do not dismiss disarmament as merely an idle dream. For we believe that, in the end, it is the only way to assure the security of all without impairing the interests of any. Nor do we mistake honorable negotiation for appeasement. While we shall never weary in the defense of freedom, neither shall we ever abandon the pursuit of peace.

In this quest, the United Nations requires our full and continued support. Its value in serving the cause of peace has been shown anew in its role in the West New Guinea settlement, in its use as a forum for the Cuban crisis, and in its task of unification in the Congo. Today the United Nations is primarily the protector of the small and the weak, and a safety valve for the strong. Tomorrow it can form the framework for a world of law - a world in which no nation dictates the destiny of another, and in which the vast resources now devoted to destructive means will serve constructive ends.

In short, let our adversaries choose. If they choose peaceful competition, they shall have it. If they come to realize that their ambitions cannot succeed - if they see their "wars of liberation" and subversion will ultimately fail - if they recognize that there is more security in accepting inspection than in permitting new nations to master the black arts of nuclear war - and if they are willing to turn their energies, as we are, to the great unfinished tasks of our own peoples - then, surely, the areas of agreement can be very wide indeed: a clear understanding about Berlin, stability in Southeast Asia, an end to nuclear testing, new checks on surprise or accidental attack, and, ultimately, general and complete disarmament.

VIII.

For we seek not the worldwide victory of one nation or system but a worldwide victory of man. The modern globe is too small, its weapons are too destructive, and its disorders are too contagious to permit any other kind of victory.

To achieve this end, the United States will continue to spend a greater portion of its national production than any other people in the free world. For 15 years no other free nation has demanded so much of itself. Through hot wars and cold, through recession and prosperity, through the ages of the atom and outer space, the American people have never faltered and their faith has never flagged. If at times our actions seem to make life difficult for others, it is only because history has made life difficult for us all.

But difficult days need not be dark. I think these are proud and memorable days in the cause of peace and freedom. We are proud, for example, of Major Rudolf Anderson who gave his life over the island of Cuba. We salute Specialist James Allen Johnson who died on the border of South Korea. We pay honor to Sergeant Gerald Pendell who was killed in Viet-Nam. They are among the many who in this century, far from home, have died for our country. Our task now, and the task of all Americans is to live up to their commitment.

My friends: I close on a note of hope. We are not lulled by the momentary calm of the sea or the somewhat clearer skies above. We know the turbulence that lies below, and the storms that are beyond the horizon this year. But now the winds of change appear to be blowing more strongly than ever, in the world of communism as well as our own. For 175 years we have sailed with those winds at our back, and with the tides of human freedom in our favor. We steer our ship with hope, as Thomas Jefferson said, "leaving Fear astern."

Today we still welcome those winds of change - and we have every reason to believe that our tide is running strong. With thanks to Almighty God for seeing us through a perilous passage, we ask His help anew in guiding the "Good Ship Union."